1·2·3 Draw

Dogs

A step-by-step guide

by Freddie Levin

Peel Productions, Inc
Vancouver, Washington

Before you begin...

You will need:

- a pencil

- an eraser

- paper (recycle and re-use)

- a pencil sharpener

- colored pencils for finished drawings

- a folder to keep your work

- a good light and a comfortable place to draw

Now, let's begin!

Published by Peel Productions, Inc.
Printed in China

Levin, Freddie.
    1-2-3 draw dogs : a step-by-step guide / by Freddie Levin.
        p. cm.
    Includes index.
    ISBN 0-939217-64-3 (trade paper : alk. paper)
    1. Drawing--Technique--Juvenile literature. 2. Dogs in art--Juvenile literature. I. Title: Draw dogs. II. Title: One-two-three draw dogs. III. Title.

    NC783.8.D64L48 2008
    743.6'9772--dc22

                2008008561

Distributed to the trade and art markets in North America by

NORTH LIGHT BOOKS,
an imprint of F&W Publications, Inc.
4700 East Galbraith Road
Cincinnati, OH 45236

(800) 289-0963

Contents

Important Drawing Tips:

1 Draw lightly at first. SKETCH, so you can easily erase extra lines later.

2 The first few shapes are important. Notice the placement, sizes, and positions of the first shapes.

3 Practice, practice, practice!

4 Have fun drawing dogs!

Basic shapes

The drawings in this book begin with three basic shapes. Learn these shapes and practice drawing them.

Circle   Oval   Egg

Note to parents and teachers:

Just like swimming, riding a bicycle, or playing the piano, drawing gets better and better with practice.

Encourage children to practice basic shapes of circles, eggs, and ovals. For very young children or children with poor motor control, cut shapes out of tag board and let them trace around them.

The size and position of the first few shapes are important. Once the beginning shapes and their positions on the page are established, the rest of the drawing can be more easily built around them.

About Dogs

Dogs come in an amazing variety of shapes and sizes. There are over 400 breeds of dogs recognized all over the world. There are big dogs, small dogs, skinny dogs, and chunky dogs. They have smooth coats, curly coats, rough wiry coats, and long silky coats. Some dogs do important jobs like herd sheep, guide the blind, or rescue people lost in the snow, and others do nothing more than live a petted pampered life. Despite this great variety, there is one thing true about all dogs. They are all descended from the wolf.

The partnership between dogs and people began around 50,000 years ago in the area that is now known as Switzerland. The earliest dogs looked a lot like the wild Australian Dingo (page 9-11). The great variety of dogs we see today developed fairly recently, in the last hundred years.

Wolf

Wolves are social animals that live in packs. They hunt together and raise their young together. The leader of the pack is called the Alpha Male. All dogs have the wolf as a common ancestor. Other relatives in this family group are jackals, foxes, and hyenas.

1 Start with a small circle for the head and an oval for the body. Look at the size and position of the shapes.

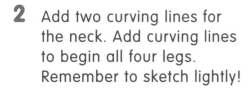

2 Add two curving lines for the neck. Add curving lines to begin all four legs. Remember to sketch lightly!

3 Draw lines for the upper and lower jaw. Add an ear. Draw the lower part of all four legs.

4 Draw the nose, eye, and inner ear. Complete the legs. Add the tail.

5   Erase extra lines.

6   Shade and color your wolf.

Wonderful wolf!

8

Dingo

Dingos are wild dogs who live in the Australian outback. Pictures of Dingos can be found in Aboriginal rock paintings, as companions to ancient spirits.

1 Start with three circles. Notice the size and position of the circles. The middle one is slightly larger.

2 Draw the muzzle. A muzzle is an animal's jaw, nose, and mouth. Connect the circles with curving lines for the neck, belly, and back.

3 Draw two ears. Add an eye, a nose, and a mouth. Draw lines to begin all four legs.

4 Complete the legs. Add a tail.

5 Draw the inner ear and finish the legs with four paws.

6 Erase extra lines. Add the other inner ear. Complete the details of the face. Add jagged lines for fur. Draw toes.

7 Shade and color your Dingo.

11

Chihuahua

Chihuahuas are the smallest of the small dogs, weighing only two to four pounds and measuring 6 to 9 inches high at the shoulders. They are from the Mexican state of the same name and in ancient times were considered sacred to the Aztecs.

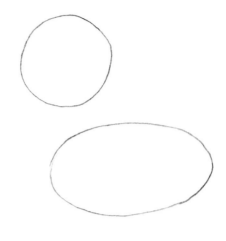

1 Draw a circle for the head and an oval for the body.

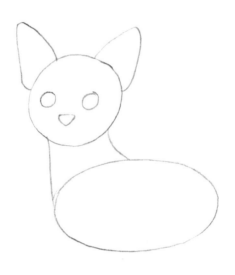

2 Add ears. Draw two eyes and a nose. Draw two curved lines for the neck.

3 Draw the inner ear. Add a tail. Using curved lines, begin all four legs.

4 Draw the muzzle and the nose. Complete all four legs.

5 Erase extra lines. Look at the face and body markings. Add lines for these.

6 Shade and color your Chihuahua.

¡Hola!

Great Dane

Great Danes are one of the tallest dogs, 32 inches high at the shoulders. Although it sounds like they are from Denmark, Great Danes developed in Germany where they were used for hunting wild boar.

1   Start with a circle and an oval. Notice the angle of the oval.

2   Add the upper and lower jaw. Draw two curving lines for the neck. Begin all four legs.

3   Draw ears, an eye, and a nose. Draw the lower part of all four legs.

4 Draw the tongue. Add an inner ear. Draw the curving tail. Add four paws.

5 Erase extra lines.

15

6 Shade and color your Great Dane.

The smallest and the tallest!

Dachshund

The Dachshund is a popular pet dog shaped like a hot dog! Dachshunds have short legs and long bodies, and are ideal for hunting burrowing animals like badgers.

1 Start with three circles. Notice that the middle circle is slightly larger.

2 Add a muzzle. Draw curving lines for the neck, belly and back.

3 Draw a nose and an eye. Add a line for the mouth. Draw an ear. Draw a tail. Begin the legs.

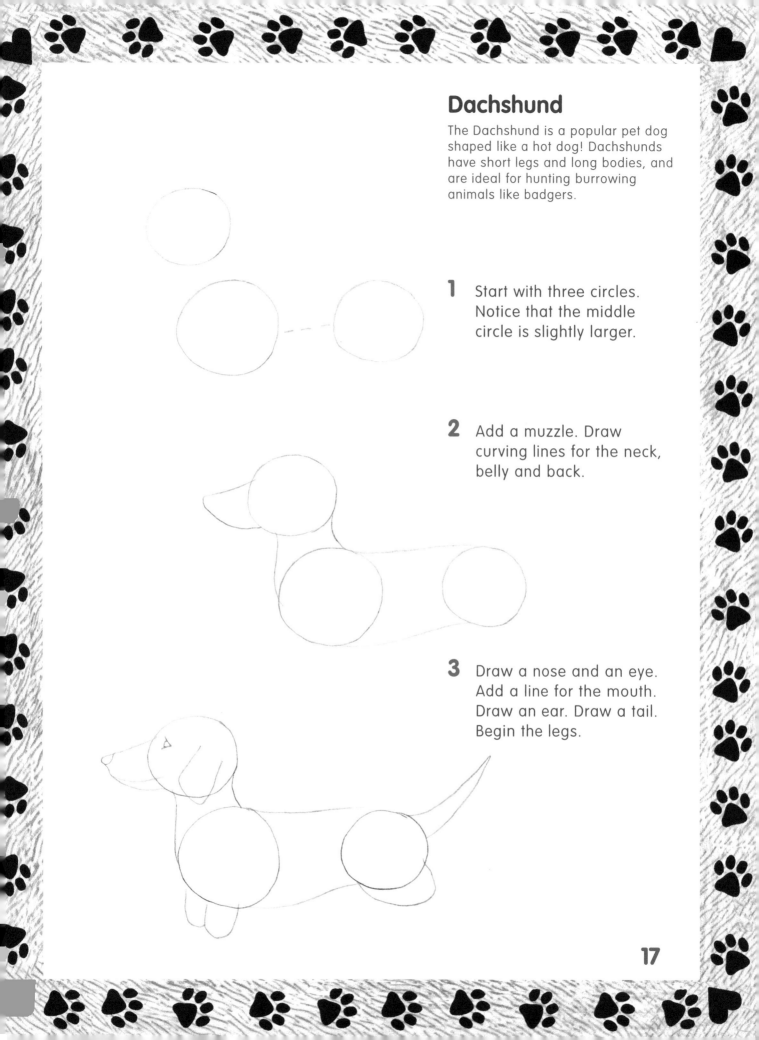

4 Complete all four legs. Add toes to the paws.

5 Erase extra lines.

6 Shade and color your dachshund.

18

West Highland Terrier

West Highland Terriers are called Westies for short. They come from the Highlands of Scotland. They are small, stocky dogs with a wiry white coat and a very merry nature.

1 Start with three circles. Notice how they overlap. Are you remembering to sketch lightly?!!

2 Add two ears. Draw two eyes and a nose. Add curving lines for the belly and back. Sketch lightly!

3 Draw the inner ears. Add the mouth. Draw a tail. Begin the legs.

19

4 Complete the Westie's short little legs.

5 With light, short pencil strokes, add the Westie's shaggy fur. Erase extra lines.

6 Shade and color your West Highland Terrier.

Wonderful Westie!

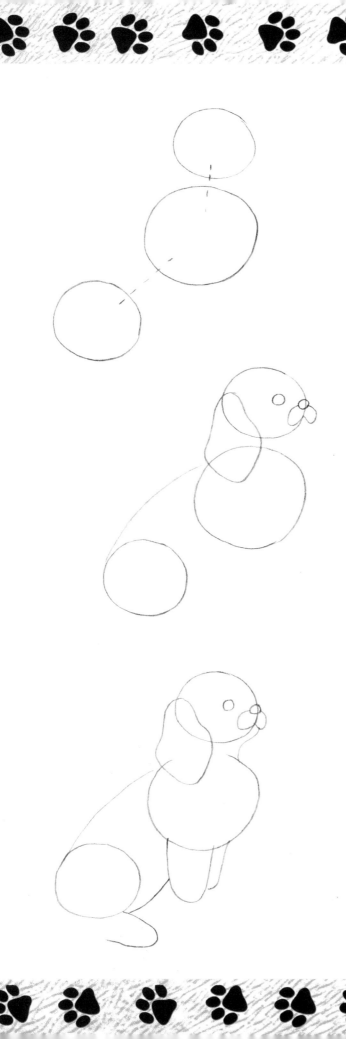

Pekinese

In ancient China, the flat faced Pekinese dog was thought to look like a little lion. Pekes lived in absolute luxury in the Emperor's palace, in the city of Peking which is now called Beijing.

1 Start with three circles. Notice the size and angle of the circles.

2 Draw an eye and a nose. Draw the muzzle. Add a floppy ear. Draw a curving line for the back.

3 Draw a curving line for a chin. Add the beginning of three legs.

21

4 Complete the legs. Add a bushy tail.

5 Erase extra lines and use short pencil strokes to show the Peke's shaggy fur.

6 Shade and color your Pekinese. Give her a satin pillow to sit on.

Pampered Peke!

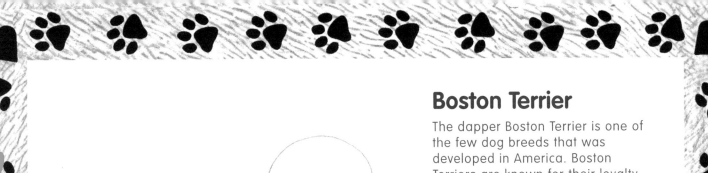

Boston Terrier

The dapper Boston Terrier is one of the few dog breeds that was developed in America. Boston Terriers are known for their loyalty and good nature, and are a particular favorite of mine.

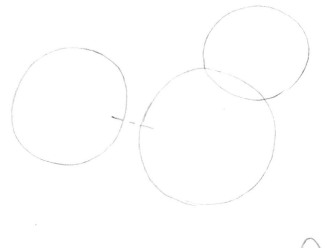

1 Start with three circles. Overlap the circle for the head.

2 Add ears and an oval for the muzzle. Draw curving lines for the belly and the back.

3 Draw two eyes and a nose. Add a tail.

23

4 Look at the mouth lines. Draw the mouth. Begin all four legs.

5 Complete the legs.

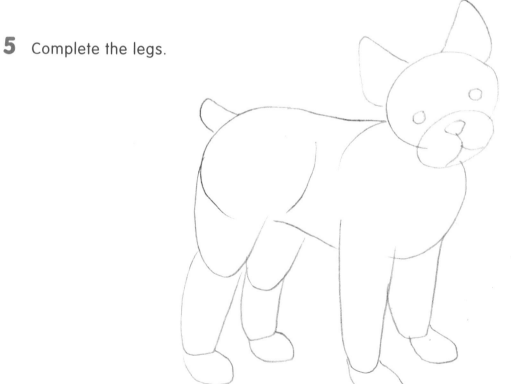

6 Look at the face, chest, and leg markings. Add these. Erase extra lines.

7 Shade and color your Boston Terrier.

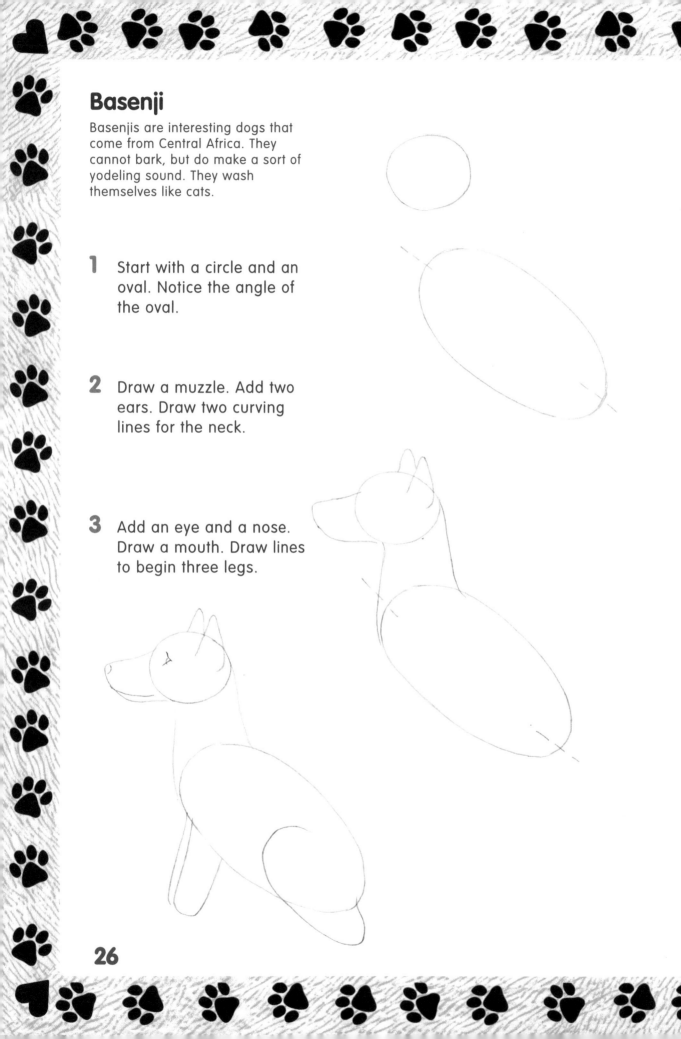

Basenji

Basenjis are interesting dogs that come from Central Africa. They cannot bark, but do make a sort of yodeling sound. They wash themselves like cats.

1 Start with a circle and an oval. Notice the angle of the oval.

2 Draw a muzzle. Add two ears. Draw two curving lines for the neck.

3 Add an eye and a nose. Draw a mouth. Draw lines to begin three legs.

26

4 Complete the legs. Draw a curling tail.

5 Erase extra lines. Look at the body and leg markings. Add these.

6 Color and complete your Basenji.

27

Welsh Corgi

The Welsh Corgi is the favorite dog of Queen Elizabeth II of England. This sturdy, short legged dog herds cattle by nipping at their heels.

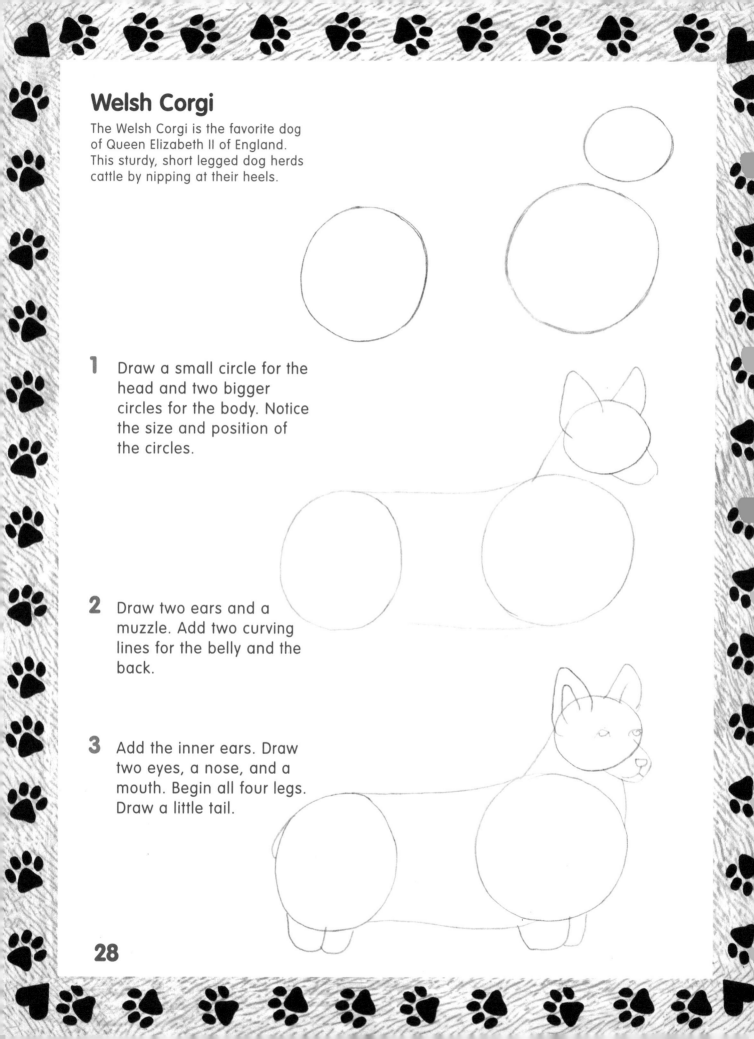

1 Draw a small circle for the head and two bigger circles for the body. Notice the size and position of the circles.

2 Draw two ears and a muzzle. Add two curving lines for the belly and the back.

3 Add the inner ears. Draw two eyes, a nose, and a mouth. Begin all four legs. Draw a little tail.

28

4 Complete the legs.

5 Erase extra lines. Draw short, shaggy lines for the fur.

6 Shade and color your Welsh Corgi.

Well done!

Dalmation

The famously spotted Dalmatian comes from the part of Eastern Europe that was once called Dalmatia. Originally used as carriage dogs, they became well known as mascots of Fire Stations. The puppies are born white and the spots begin appearing after three weeks.

1 Start with three circles. Notice the size and position of the circles.

2 Add a muzzle. Draw curving lines for the neck, belly, and back.

3 Draw a nose and an eye. Add an ear. Draw the tail.

4 Add curving lines to begin all four legs.

5 Look at the shapes that form the lower part of the legs. Draw these.

6 Erase extra lines.

7 Shade and color your Dalmation. Notice that the spots are not just little circles but small, irregular blobs.

Golden Retriever

The Golden Retriever is one of the most loved dogs in all the world. Developed in Scotland as a hunting dog by Lord Tweedmouth, it is known for its gentle, loving nature as an ideal family dog.

1 Start with three circles. Notice their size and position.

2 Draw a muzzle. Add a nose and an eye. Draw an ear. Draw a curving line for the back. Begin two front legs.

3 Complete the two front legs. Draw a back leg.

4 Erase extra lines. Use short, light pencil strokes to show the soft fur.

5 Shade and color your Golden Retriever.

34

Saint Bernard

The Saint Bernard was originally bred in the seventeenth century by the monks of the Hospice of Saint Bernard, in the Swiss Alps, as a rescue dog. This big dog, weighing up to two hundred pounds, has a unique ability to find people buried in snow. The most famous Saint Bernard was called Barry. Barry lived from 1900 to 1912 and rescued forty people during his lifetime.

1   Start with a small circle and a large oval.

2   Draw curving lines for the neck, back and belly.

3   Draw a muzzle. Add an eye and an ear. Erase extra lines.

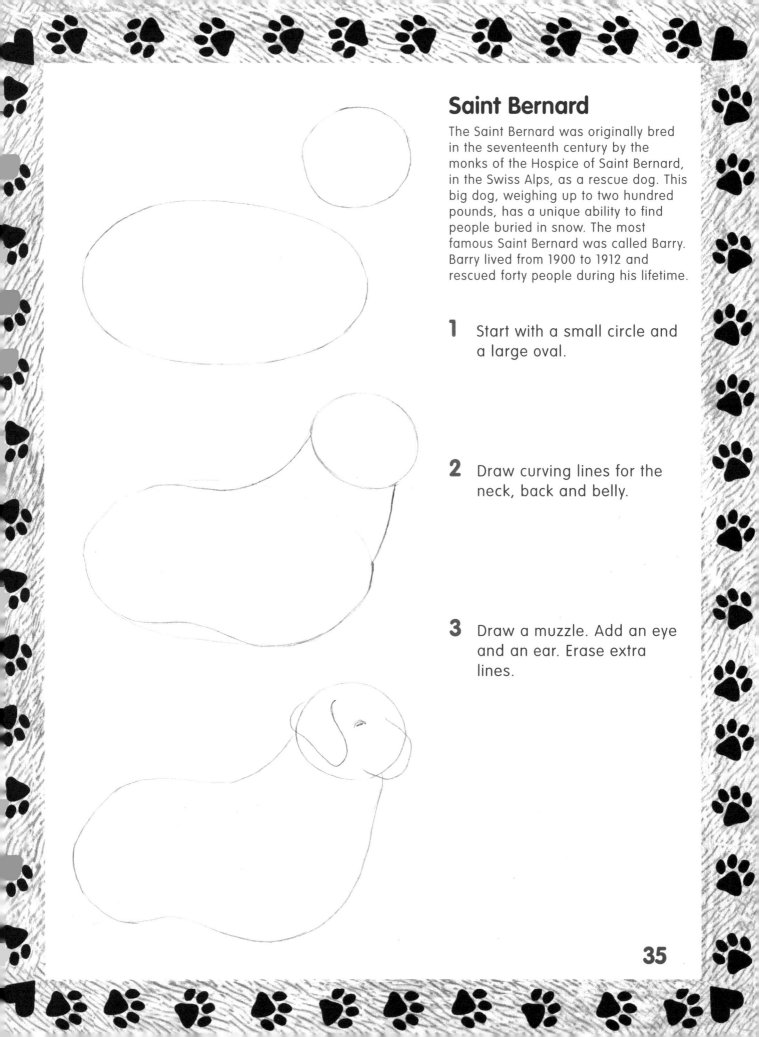

35

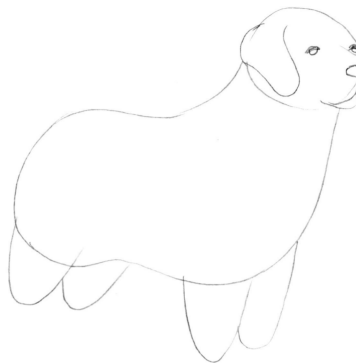

4 Draw the nose. Add a
second eye. Draw the
mouth. Begin all four legs.

5 Look at the lower part of
the legs. Add these shapes.
Draw a tail.

6 Erase extra lines. Add the markings you see.

7 Shade and color your Saint Bernard.

Super!

German Shorthaired Pointer

The German Shorthaired Pointer is an all purpose hunting dog who tracks and retrieves on land and on water. The characteristic pointing pose is so instinctive, Pointer pups will "point" at squirrels and bees even when they are very young. The Pointer is also a wonderful family pet.

1 Start with three circles. Notice their size and position.

2 Draw the muzzle. Draw curving lines for the neck, back, and belly.

3 Draw a nose and an eye. Add an ear. Begin a front leg and a back leg.

38

4 Draw a tail. Look at the the bent front leg. Draw it and the lower part of the back leg. Draw another back leg.

5 Draw the second front leg. Add feet to the back legs.

39

6 Erase extra lines. Look at the markings. Draw these.

7 Color and shade your Pointer.

Afghan Hound

As its name suggests, the Afghan Hound is from Afghanistan. The Afghan is a sight hound which means it tracks by sight rather than scent. The beautiful, longhaired coat protects it from harsh weather and requires a lot of care.

1 Start with a small circle and two larger circles. Notice the position of the circles.

2 Draw the muzzle. Add curving lines for the back and belly.

3 Draw a nose. Add a mouth. Add an eye. Draw a long floppy ear. Add a curly tail.

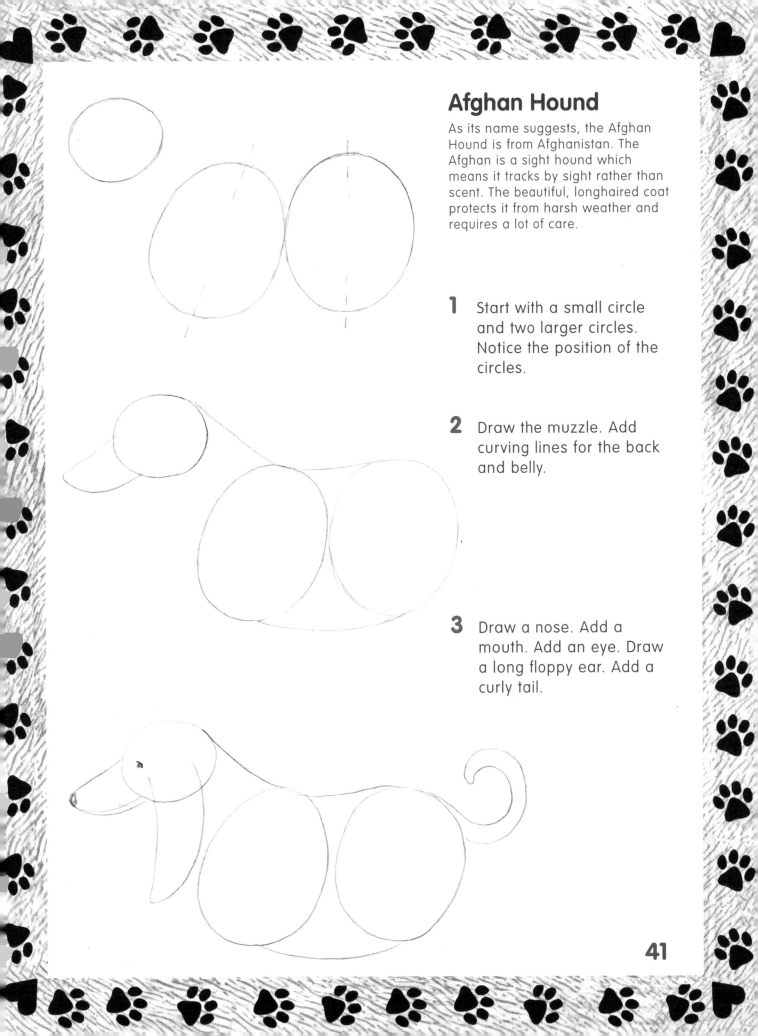

41

4 Begin all four legs.

5 Complete the legs. Erase extra lines.

6 Draw long, wavy lines to show the Afghan's unusual coat.

7 Shade and color your Afghan hound.

Awesome!

43

Greyhound

The Greyhound is the fastest dog, racing up to forty miles per hour. The Greyhound is also a sight hound and a very old breed. Pictures of Greyhounds are found in ancient Egyptian carvings.

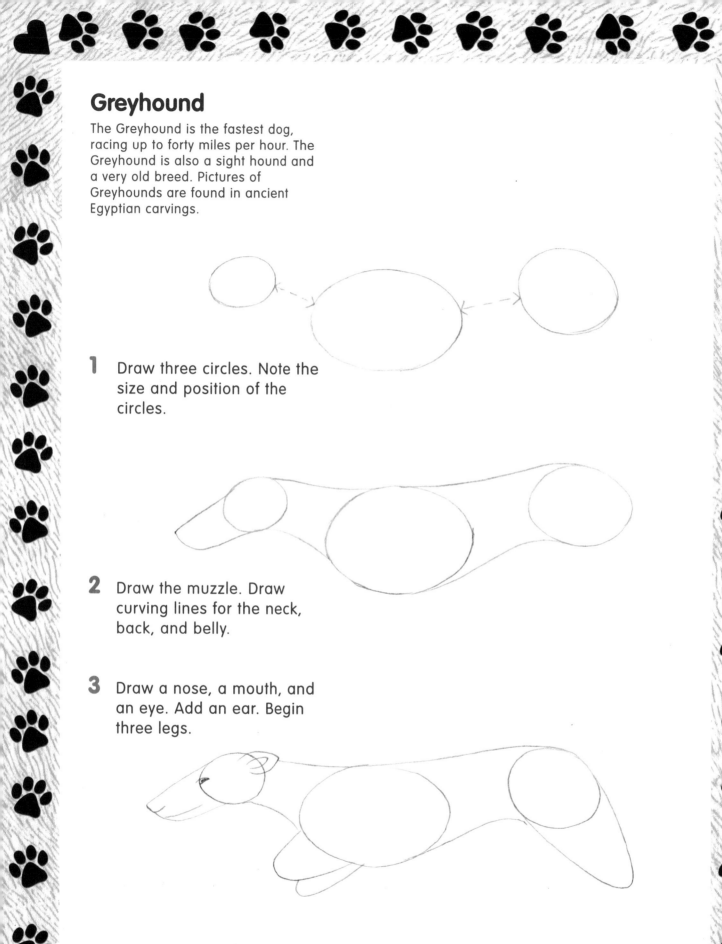

1 Draw three circles. Note the size and position of the circles.

2 Draw the muzzle. Draw curving lines for the neck, back, and belly.

3 Draw a nose, a mouth, and an eye. Add an ear. Begin three legs.

4 Complete the three legs.
   Add the second back leg.
   Draw the tail.

5 Erase extra lines.

6 Shade and color your
   Greyhound.

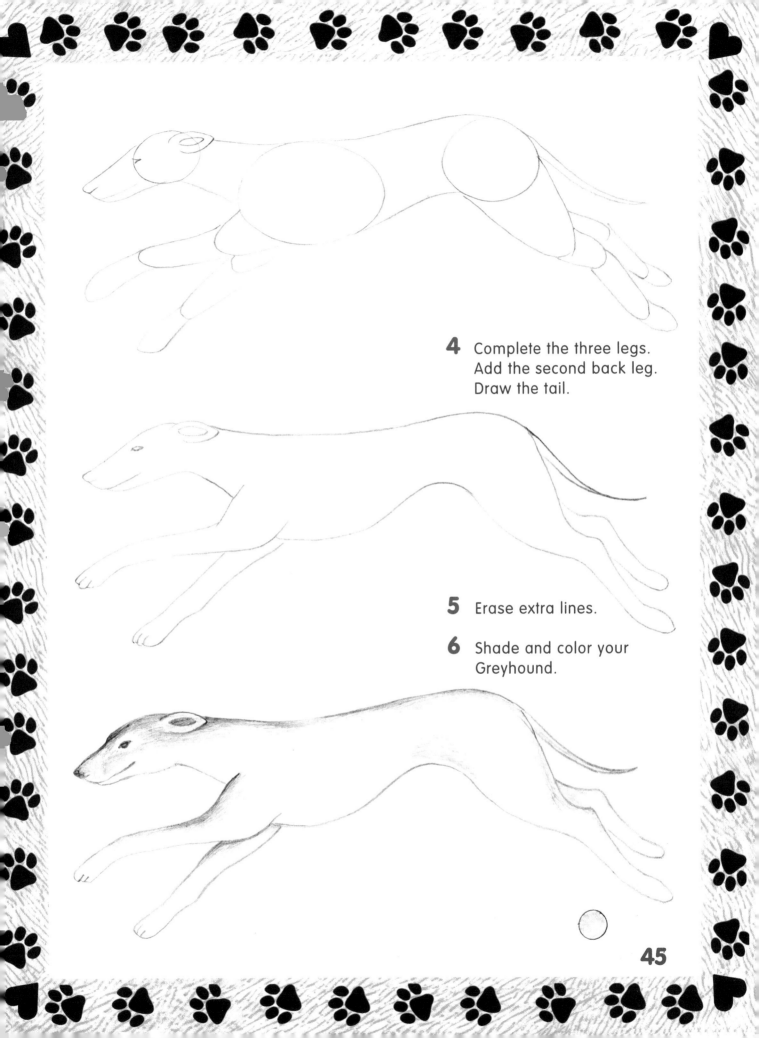

Circus Dog

Some dogs love to perform. Small dogs like terriers are often used in circuses. This little dog is part of a clown act. When he is not performing he lives with the clown who is also his trainer.

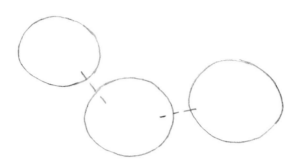

1 Start with three circles.

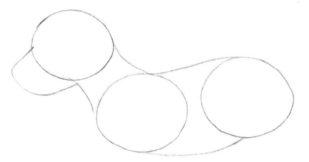

2 Draw the muzzle. Add curving lines for the neck, back and belly.

3 Draw a nose and two eyes. Add ears. Begin two front legs and a back leg.

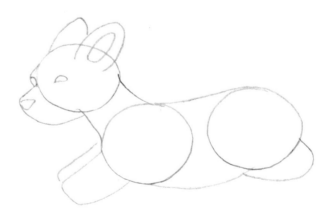

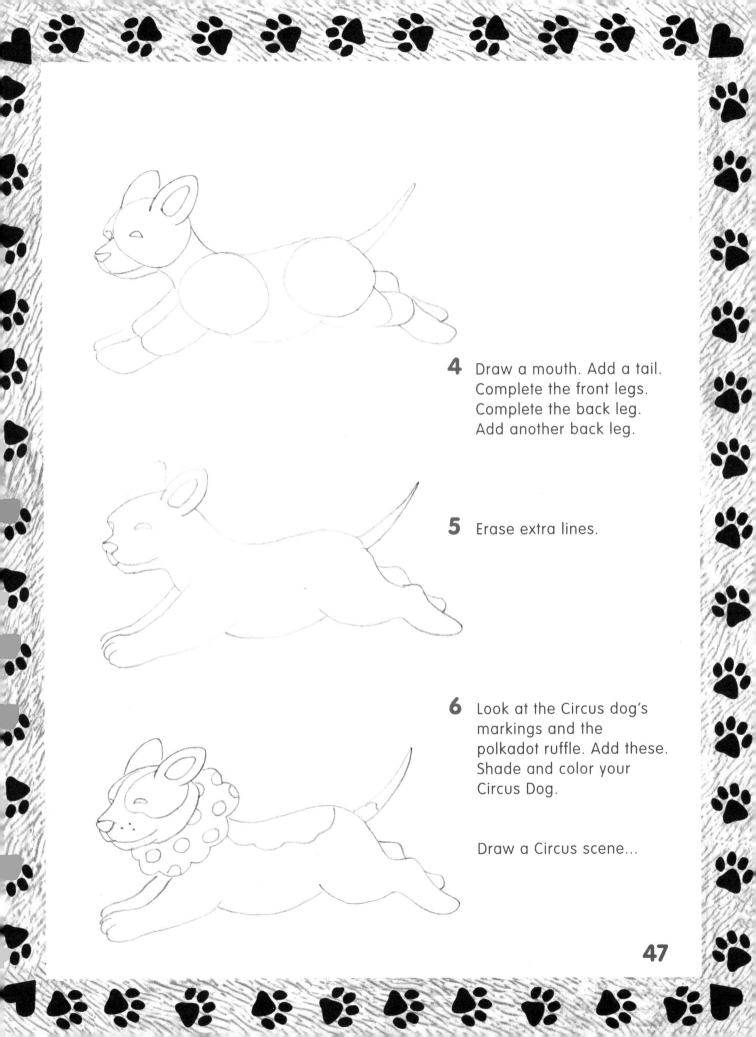

4 Draw a mouth. Add a tail. Complete the front legs. Complete the back leg. Add another back leg.

5 Erase extra lines.

6 Look at the Circus dog's markings and the polkadot ruffle. Add these. Shade and color your Circus Dog.

Draw a Circus scene...

47

48

Collie

Collies were originally bred in northern Scotland as sheepdogs. One Collie, Lassie (and a series of look-alike Lassies), became famous all over the world, starring in movies and TV shows.

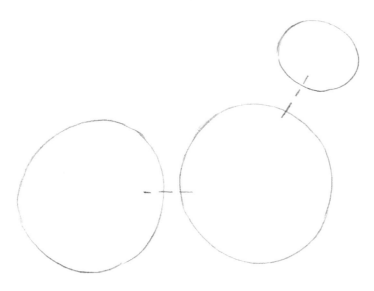

1 Start with a small circle and two large circles.

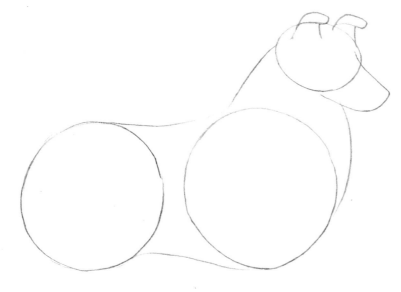

2 Draw the muzzle and two ears. Add curving lines for the neck, back and belly.

49

3 Draw an eye and a nose.
Add a mouth. Draw lines to
begin the four legs.

4 Complete the four legs.
Draw a bushy tail.

50

5 Erase extra lines. Use short, light pencil strokes to draw the Collie's shaggy coat.

6 Shade and color your collie.

What a Star!

Siberian Husky

The Siberian Husky was originally bred by the Chukchi people of Eastern Siberia. The Husky is a strong dog that can withstand harsh weather and is well known as a sled dog.

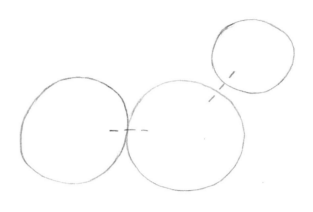

1 Start with one small circle and two large circles. Notice how the large circles are touching.

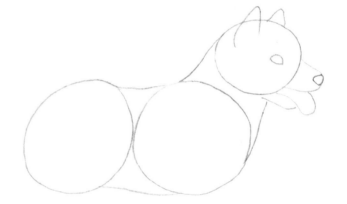

2 Draw an eye and two ears. Draw the muzzle. Draw a nose and a tongue. Add curving lines for the neck, back and belly.

3 Draw the beginning of four legs.

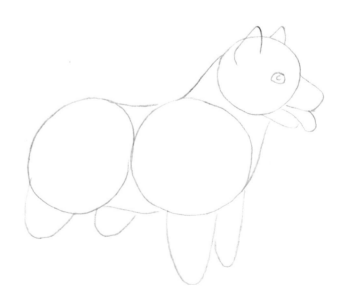

4 Complete the legs. Add a bushy tail.

5 Use light pencil strokes to draw the Husky's rough coat. Erase extra lines.

6 Shade and color your Husky.

Guide Dog for the Blind

The first guide dog for the blind was a German Shepherd named Buddy. Her success in 1920 started the movement to train dogs to help people with disabilities. German Shepherds are prized as guide dogs for their loyalty, courage, and intelligence.

First we will draw the dog. Then we will add the person she is helping.

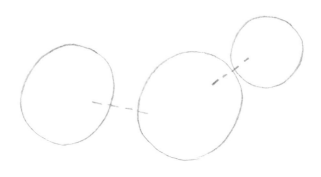

1   Draw three circles. Note the size and position of the circles.

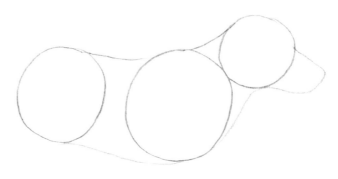

2   Draw the muzzle. Add curving lines for the neck, back, and belly.

3   Draw two ears. Draw an eye, a nose, and a mouth. Begin all four legs.

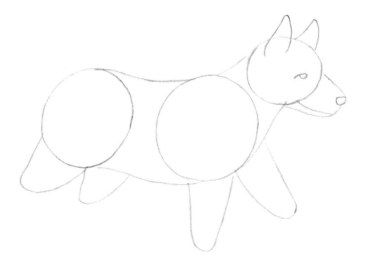

4 Draw the inner ears. Complete all four legs. Add a tail.

5 Erase extra lines.

6 Draw the special harness that Guide Dogs wear.

55

7 Draw an egg for the person's head. Add a line for the shoulder. Draw an arm.

8 Draw glasses. Add a nose and a mouth. Look at the lines that form the upper body. Draw these. Add a hand.

9 Draw a hat and hair. Add fingers to the hand. Draw the other arm and hand. Draw a skirt.

10 Look at the harness handle. Draw it.

11 Look carefully at the final drawing! What's missing? Draw the legs, shoes, and harness. Shade and color your Guide Dog and person.

Border Collie

A Border Collie is a smaller cousin to the Collie. An amazing sheepdog, it originated in the border country between Scotland and England. They are highly intelligent, energetic working dogs. If they don't have sheep to herd, they sure love to run in flyball races or catch a frisbee.

1 Start with three circles. Notice the size and position of the circles.

2 Add curving lines for the neck and belly.

3 Draw the muzzle and tongue. Add two ears and an eye.

4 Draw a nose. Begin four legs.

5 Look at the angles of the legs. Complete the four legs. Add a tail.

6 Erase extra lines. Use light pencil strokes to draw the Border Collie's coat.

7 Shade and color your Border Collie. Give him a Frisbee to catch.

Mutt

My dog Maggie was a Mutt. That means she was an unknown mix of several breeds. It must have been a great combination because for me Maggie was just the best and smartest dog in the whole wide world.

1 Start with three circles.

2 Draw the muzzle. Add curving lines for the neck and the back.

3 Add an eye and an ear. Begin two front legs.

4 Complete front legs. Draw two back legs. Add a tail.

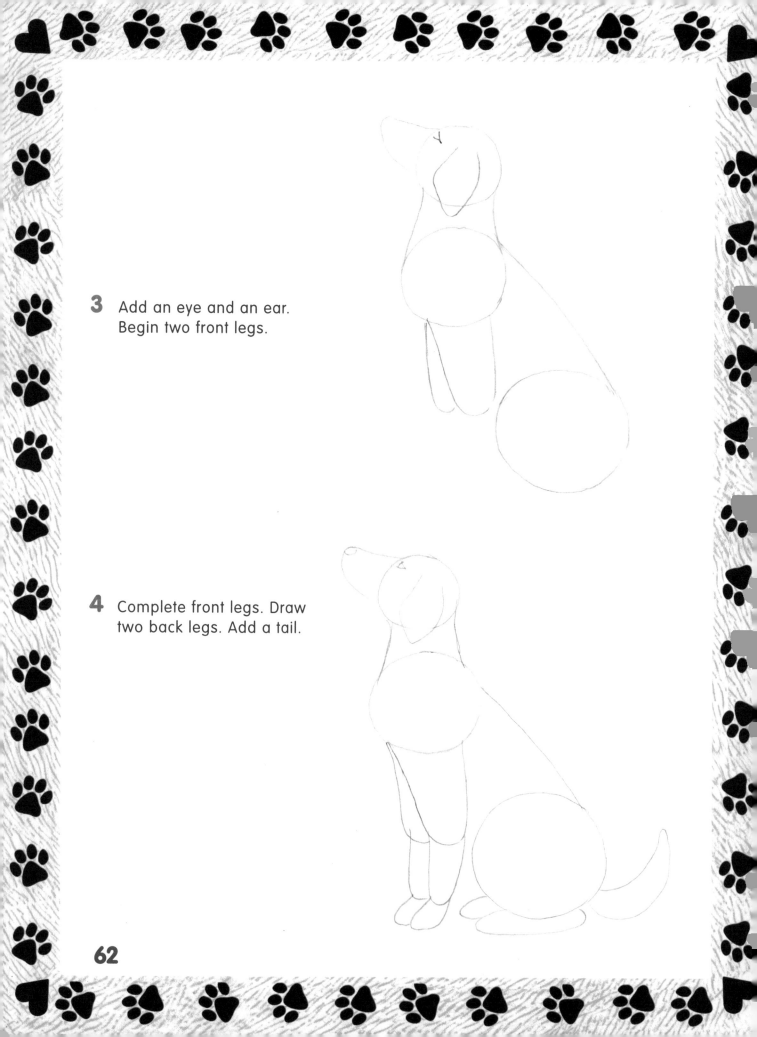

5 Erase extra lines. Use short pencil strokes to show the shaggy coat.

6 Shade and color Maggie.

Good dog! Maggie, good girl!

INDEX

Learn about other
drawing books online at
www.123draw.com